WILLIAM MORRIS
AND
MORRIS & C<u>o</u>.

WILLIAM MORRIS
AND
MORRIS & Co.

Lucia van der Post

with an introduction by Linda Parry

V&A Publications
Published in association with Arthur Sanderson & Sons Ltd
Distributed by Harry N. Abrams, Inc., Publishers

First published by V&A Publications, in association
with Arthur Sanderson & Sons Ltd, 2003

V&A Publications
160 Brompton Road, London SW3 1HW

Distributed in North America
by Harry N. Abrams, Incorporated, New York

Designed by Nigel Soper
Project management by Geoff Barlow
Printed in Hong Kong

ISBN 0-8109-6612-3 (Harry N. Abrams, Inc)
Library of Congress Control Number 2003106302

A catalogue record for this book is available
from the British Library.

Arthur Sanderson & Sons Ltd
Sanderson House
Denham, England
www.sanderson-uk.com

Harry N. Abrams, Inc
100 Fifth Avenue
New York, N.Y. 10011
www.abramsbooks.com

Contents

Author's Acknowledgements

The author gratefully acknowledges the various published sources that have been invaluable during her research into the life and work of William Morris. In particular she would like to thank Linda Parry of the Victoria and Albert Museum for advice on many detailed points, and for contributing the historical introduction.

The book owes its current shape and form to the work of many individuals, among whom I would especially like to thank: Mary Butler, Head of V&A Publications; Geoff Barlow, V&A Publications project manager; Rachel Connolly, for her meticulous copy-editing and proofreading; Freddie Launert, for her diligence in researching and gathering the varied images to illustrate the text; and Nigel Soper for his inspired layout and design.

RIGHT: *Trial printing of* IRIS *furnishing textile. Designed by William Morris, registered April 1876.*

INTRODUCTION

WILLIAM MORRIS WAS BORN IN WALTHAMSTOW in 1834 into an affluent middle-class family. He was educated at Marlborough and Exeter College, Oxford, and it was here that he first developed a great interest in art and literature. With such conventional beginnings, it is hardly surprising that his interests did not lie with fashionable Victorian paintings and books, but that instead he developed a passion for all things Gothic; not only for thirteenth- and fourteenth-century English and French architecture and decoration, but for the high ideals and principles of chivalrous life. This was, in many ways, an escape from Victorian industrial society, which he found unattractive and destructive. Influenced by the writings of contemporary critics such as Thomas Carlyle, Charles Kingsley and, in particular, John Ruskin, he saw the benefits of returning to the working patterns of medieval England, where guilds were set up to monitor work and the conditions and pay of workers. These ideals stayed with him throughout his life as a designer, manufacturer, writer and political activist.

On leaving Oxford in 1856 and after a short spell in an architectural practice, Morris began to paint, but his talents as a designer soon became evident. Sharing a flat in London with his close college friend Edward Burne-Jones, the two began to make furniture and decorate their home in a novel and interesting way, producing decorative effects quite unlike anything available in the shops at that time.

In 1859 Morris married Jane Burden, and the decoration of their newly built home, Red House, in Bexleyheath, Kent, gave Morris and his friends further opportunities to design and make furnishings as part of an entire decorative scheme. Although the house interior was thought 'weird' by more conventional visitors, many admired the decorations and, with no comparable goods for sale, Morris and his friends were encouraged to develop their work as a commercial venture. On 11 April 1861, Morris, Marshall, Faulkner and Company was formed with eight partners. Premises were taken in Red Lion Square (later moving to Queen Square), London, and the company's first products were mural decorations, architectural carvings, stained

ABOVE: *A photograph of William Morris, c. 1875.*

ABOVE RIGHT: *Wallpaper sample,* DAISY. *Designed by William Morris, registered 1864.*

RIGHT: *Wallpaper sample,* FRUIT *(or* POMEGRANATE*). Designed by William Morris, first issued c. 1866.*

glass, metalwork and furniture. At the International Exhibition of 1862 held in South Kensington, they exhibited stained glass, furniture and embroidered hangings, and, as well as selling £150 worth of goods, were presented with two gold medals.

As manager, Morris was the main inspirational and artistic force behind production. In time, some of the partners left either to develop independent careers or because they were simply no longer happy to be part of a company dominated by Morris. The partnership was dissolved and soon afterwards, in 1875, reorganized as Morris and Company under Morris's sole proprietorship. In 1877 the shop moved to Oxford Street and soon became an important focal point for fashionable London.

Morris's ambitions as a designer and manufacturer were great, and his desire to improve the general standard of interior design and methods and conditions of production led him to experiment at one time or another with the design and

LEFT: *Wallpaper sample,* LARKSPUR. *Designed by William Morris, first issued c. 1872.*

ABOVE: *The carpet-weaving workshop at Merton Abbey.*

manufacture of all domestic furnishings: ceramic tiles, glass, metalwork, woodwork, and all types of textiles and wallpapers. Whereas techniques involving simple processes and equipment were perfected in the early years of production, textiles were at first restricted to embroidery, which did not involve complicated equipment or the supply of expensive and scarce raw materials. Nevertheless, textiles and wallpapers were considered from the earliest an important part of his schemes as an interior designer and manufacturer. Their production could not be compromised, however, and Morris was not prepared to use quick, modern machine methods of printing and cheap dyestuffs in order to speed up production. Between 1862 and 1866, Morris drew three repeating patterns for wallpaper: *Daisy, Trellis* and *Fruit* (also called *Pomegranate*). He then attempted to print these by engraving the patterns onto zinc plates. The results were far from satisfactory and he turned to a London wallpaper manufacturer, Jeffrey and Company of Islington, for advice. He could not have been more fortunate in this for the managing director of Jeffrey's was Metford Warner, a man of great artistic sensitivity. Jeffrey & Co. used modern distemper colours in their own production but, with the masterly mixing of colours and careful use of woodblocks, Warner convinced Morris that the results they obtained were better than anything Morris could produce himself. From this time Morris entrusted the production of all Morris & Co. wallpapers to the Islington firm. Pattern books now owned by Sanderson's show samples of these early designs and the painstaking trials that were involved.

Between 1875 and 1880, Morris concentrated on the production of printed and woven textiles and at first employed outside firms to print and weave his designs. He spent weeks working alongside Thomas Wardle in his Print Works in Leek, Staffordshire, attempting to revive a number of forgotten vegetable printing and dyeing techniques – indigo blue and madder red, for instance – and Morris's first twelve printed textile designs were block-printed with vegetable dyes at Wardle's factory. Within time, silk, cotton, wool and linen fabrics were woven for the company by a number of established firms in Cheshire, Lancashire and Yorkshire.

In 1881 Morris moved a major part of his production to a disused factory at Merton Abbey on the River Wandle between Wandsworth and Wimbledon. Here, in the weatherboarded buildings, he set up a stained-glass workshop and departments dealing with the dyeing of yarns, the weaving and printing of fabrics, the hand-knotting of carpets, and eventually the weaving of tapestries. In 1885 Morris's younger daughter May took over management of the embroidery section of the firm, which, like furniture production, remained in London.

Despite a reputation as a dreamer and idealist, recent research has proved that Morris was a clever and astute businessman. This is shown through the gradual nurturing of an enterprise that, from modest and humble beginnings, became a firm with an international reputation. However, his skill as an original and versatile pattern designer played no small part in the firm's commercial success, which, by

the mid-1880s, was at its height. The development of Morris's patterns, from early medieval-inspired wallpapers to subtle repeating designs of English garden flowers drawn ten years later for wallpapers and printed textiles, shows his increasing preoccupation with nature and a growing confidence in his own intuitive powers as a pattern designer and botanical draughtsman. His attitude towards patterns was practical, however, adapting each for the technique for which it was intended, and his designs for printed and woven textiles, wallpapers and machine-woven carpets are all quite different. Occasionally an exception to this rule was made, and three patterns – *Tulip*, *Marigold* and *Larkspur* – were designed for use as wallpapers and printed textiles. These designs have proved popular in recent years when used as part of a co-ordinated scheme.

As a collector of historic textiles, Morris's admiration for traditional repeating

ABOVE: MARIGOLD *furnishing textile. Designed by William Morris, registered as a wallpaper in February 1875, and as a textile on 15 April 1875.*

ABOVE: BROTHER RABBIT
printed cotton. Designed by
William Morris, 1880–1.

ABOVE RIGHT: *Wallpaper*
sample, BIRD AND ANEMONE.
Designed by William Morris,
first issued 1882.

methods increased, and his mature patterns show floral patterns in a traditional framework. His most characteristic designs are those of the early 1880s, showing symmetrical repeating pairs of British wild animals and birds. Two monochrome designs, *Brother Rabbit* and *Bird and Anemone*, are not sentimentalized despite their subject matter, and have a freshness and humour not seen in the original seventeenth-century Italian woven silks on which they are based.

By the late 1880s, Morris's various activities outside Merton Abbey began to monopolize his time, and in 1890 he took on two business partners who took over responsibility for the shop. The management of the Merton Abbey Works was left to Morris's assistant, John Henry Dearle. Originally recruited by Morris & Co. in 1878 to work in the shop, Morris soon recognized Dearle's potential as a designer and he was subsequently trained as a tapestry weaver. By 1890 he was producing all

THESE PAPERS ARE
PRINTED BY HAND

Hand or Block-printed Papers and Machine-printed Papers.

MORRIS AND COMPANY are often asked "What is the advantage of hand-printed papers over those printed by machine?"
HAND-PRINTED PAPERS are produced very slowly, each block used being dipped into pigment and then firmly pressed on to the paper, giving a great body of colour. This process takes place with each separate colour, which is slowly dried before another is applied. The consequence is that in the finished paper there is a considerable mass of solid colour.
MACHINE-PRINTED PAPERS are produced at a great speed, all the colours being printed at one time and rapidly dried in a heated gallery. In consequence of the speed at which they are printed, there is merely a film of colour deposited on the surface of the paper.
FOR PERMANENT USE we strongly recommend the hand-printed papers.

The machine-printed papers are placed at the end of one of the books or in a small book by themselves.

Show Rooms:
449, Oxford Street, London, W.

LEFT: *Wallpaper stand book from Morris & Co., 449 Oxford Street, c. 1905.*

the new designs for the company's stained glass, wallpapers, textiles, carpets and tapestries. At first Dearle's designs showed the strong influence of Morris's work, but he soon developed his own individual style, often working on a larger scale than Morris had done, but just as attractive in colour and pattern. By restricting his designs to show birds, trees, flowers and shrubs, Dearle continued the tradition established by Morris and helped maintain the firm's popularity well into the twentieth century.

With Morris's untimely death in 1896, no immediate change was seen in production, but by the end of the nineteenth century Morris's patterns had begun to fall out of fashion. The firm found it hard to compete with the new patterns and styles of interior design becoming increasingly popular in Britain, and in 1905 a board of directors was set up with the aim of reviving the past popularity of the firm through modernization. With the exception of Dearle, now the artistic director, the new board consisted of businessmen with no artistic training whatsoever, and soon the firm's products showed attempts to compete with the fashionable Edwardian market, turning away from its own original and timeless style. At first they were successful, but a gradual diminishing of the workforce and difficulties in the supply of raw materials for production in the years leading up to the First World War caused the closure of a large section of the Merton Abbey Works. Despite valiant attempts to revive manufacture and look for new outlets, Morris & Co. never fully recovered. It became increasingly difficult to find the vegetable dyes so important for the production of textiles, and a general compromise in the high standards demanded by Morris showed in many of the unsatisfactory products of the 1930s. With Dearle's death in 1932 and the gradual onset of war at the end of the decade, it became clear that the firm was unable to produce or sell enough goods to survive in a very competitive market. On 21 March 1940 the firm went into voluntary liquidation.

ABOVE: ACORN *wallpaper by William Morris, 1879.*

Morris patterns have continued to be successfully printed since that time by two firms who inherited the rights to Morris & Co.'s patterns through being early contractors of the firm. Jeffrey & Co. continued to print Morris wallpapers into the early twentieth century, when they were taken over by the Wallpaper Manufacturers Ltd. WPM continued this contract work until Morris & Co. closed. The blocks were then allocated to the Perivale factory of Arthur Sanderson & Sons, rightly regarded as the successor to Jeffrey & Co. Similarly, the Carlisle printers Stead McAlpin, who had produced many printed textiles for Morris & Co. in the late nineteenth and early twentieth centuries, acquired the stock of textile printing blocks.

From the 1950s, Sanderson's range of hand-block printed Morris wallpapers have been in constant production, and some Morris designs have been transferred to machine, providing a more accessible range of surface-printed papers. The firm has also been responsible for issuing a number of Morris wallpaper patterns as printed cottons and linens. The popularity of Morris designs has not waned in the last fifty years. In fact his skills as one of the most versatile and talented of all British pattern designers is appreciated more today than at any time in the past.

CRAFT

I

CRAFT
a revival of traditional skills

IN THE SUMMER OF 1880, when he was forty-six, William Morris wrote to his wife Janey from their London home:

> Breakfast is over and I have been carpeteering: the Orchard, spread out on the drawing room floor, though not perfect as a piece of manufacture is not amiss; as a work of art I am a little disappointed with it: if I do it again it shall have a wider border I think. . . The 3 yellow bordered pots are not so flat as they should be: I fear the worsted warp is to blame for this: I shall use cotton in future, and perhaps dye it blue roughly.

Here is one of the most highly regarded interior designers of the Victorian age, the great purveyor of textiles, tiles, furniture and 'every article necessary for domestic use' to a style-conscious elite, on his hands and knees, nose-deep in carpet pile, quizzing every knot. It is an endearing image.

Amusing as the image is, it holds the key to Morris's contemporary success and his continuing significance to all those interested in harmonious domestic interiors. This carpet had been hand-knotted to Morris's own design by women brought in to work in the coach house attached to his Hammersmith home. The design and making processes were brought together as closely as possible, both of them located in as congenial and nearly domestic a setting as possible. The carpet itself was the latest product of Morris's appetite for hands-on, practical experimenting and for exhaustive research into traditional techniques. It represented both the culmination of a deeply personal childhood love of oriental carpets and the manufacturer's professional ambition to supply truly well-made products 'which may claim to be considered works of art'. Above all, it is a wonderful demonstration of how craft, the minutiae of making, far from being the despised other half of the more exalted task of designing, was the central passion of Morris's life. Whether the process involved, as in this case, actual handwork, or whether it involved the use of simple machines, what mattered to Morris was that the product was the very best of its kind, the most beautiful and most skilfully made from the most appropriate and most satisfying materials.

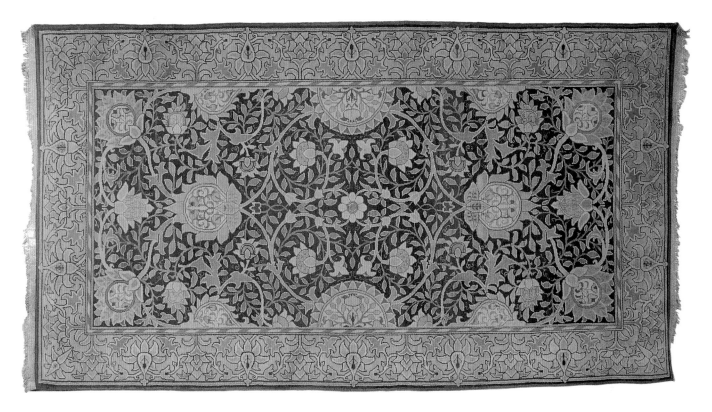

ABOVE: *A traditionally hand-knotted carpet, designed by Morris in 1881–3 and woven in 1883–4 for the antiquities room of A.A. Ionides' house at 1 Holland Park. For Morris, hand techniques never suggested the amateurish or second-rate but were in fact employed for the most prestigious pieces.*

Today the word craft, in the sense of skilful making, has become virtually synonymous with handicraft, or making by hand, individually. The one-off piece of studio pottery or woven fabric made by a named artist-craftsman is a cult object, and 'handmade' has become a much-abused shorthand for high quality. This wasn't so for Morris. In his commitment to finding the best possible way to produce beautiful wallpapers, textiles, carpets or furniture, he was prepared to explore any technique and system of manufacture. However, he had a deeply held emotional prejudice towards the artisan, the skilled craftsman, as the ideal figure of the maker, and was in favour of the local, the domestic, the native and natural as the most congenial environment and materials for the production of work of the highest quality. In the middle of the nineteenth century, in the heyday of our love affair with the machine and industrial processing, this position was considered by many to be deeply eccentric.

As the sulky seventeen-year-old heir to a City fortune, William Morris had refused to enter the Crystal Palace to see the Great Exhibition with his family. He already had a horror of the meretricious furniture and decoration that 'new money', such as his father's, had made fashionable. It was only when he got to Oxford, however, that he found the intellectual armoury that helped him articulate his distaste.

In his great book on medieval art and architecture, *The Stones of Venice*, and above all in his stirring chapter 'On the Nature of Gothic Architecture: and herein of the true functions of the workman in art', the writer John Ruskin blamed the degradation

LEFT: *Simple, well-made designs, such as these classic Morris chairs, work well in present-day interiors.*

BELOW: *Morris's belief that work should, as far as possible, be an integral part of life, as opposed to a thing apart, is beautifully exemplified by this pretty courtyard, where it is hard to tell which pots are on sale and which are part of the garden, or where the home ends and the sale room begins.*

RIGHT: *A Morris, Marshall, Faulkner & Co. tile, decorated with PRIMROSE pattern. Inspired by 18th-century Dutch and English tin-glazed tiles, for Morris such tiles evoked a simple domesticity that he loved.*

ABOVE: *The conservatory of Emery Walker's house at 7 Hammersmith Terrace. A typical Arts and Crafts interior, bringing together highly decorated pottery, a Morris print, a traditional ladder-back chair and a growing vine to create a relaxed and homely corner of the house, filled with light.*

of modern taste on the enslavement of workmen to industrial process. Ruskin was sure that 'the difference between the spirit of touch of the man who is inventing, and of the man who is obeying directions, is often all the difference between a great and a common work of art'. He believed that the solution lay in the revival of handcrafts and the abolition of false distinctions between the designer and the maker, the artist and the craftsman.

For Morris, Ruskin's analysis struck home. It was a revelation. It confirmed and articulated his deepest instincts. 'To some of us when we first read it, now many years ago, it seemed to point out a new road on which the world should travel.' His Oxford friends were subjected to prolonged and passionate readings from Ruskin, and Morris abandoned his earlier ambition to found a monastic order and took an apprenticeship as an architect instead.

It was from Ruskin that Morris derived his own abiding principle: 'That thing which I understand by real art is the expression by man of his pleasure in labour. I do not believe he can be happy in his labour without expressing that happiness; and especially this is so when he is at work at anything in which he specially excels.' Potentially, this had profound political implications, as Morris's many years as a revolutionary socialist testify. More universally, however, it points to a quality that is hard to put your finger on but that is undeniably there in all great work, whether it be a painting, a pot, a roll of wallpaper or a fine tapestry — an inherent quality that derives from the pride, expertise and creative freedom of its maker. It gives craft or good workmanship, and the pleasure we take in it, a moral dimension, so that it is no longer a purely sensory phenomenon.

For over forty years Morris never abandoned his belief in the virtues of craftsmanship, maintaining an intensely personal relationship with the processes he was interested in. Even as an apprentice architect under G.E. Street, himself an enthusiastic designer of embroideries, Morris threw himself energetically into clay modelling, wood carving and stone carving. He started making his first illuminated manuscripts. After the move to London, in the chaotic premises in Red Lion Square that he inhabited with Edward Burne-Jones, Morris taught himself embroidery. Soon he added mural painting, tile painting, dyeing, wood engraving and calligraphy to his tally of skills and adopted, as a badge of honour, the blue working shirt of the artisan. Perhaps his greatest love, though, was tapestry weaving, which he took up in the 1870s and never abandoned. When business became pressured he would long for his loom: 'Lord bless us how nice it will be when I can get back to my little patterns and dyeing, and the dear warp and weft at Hammersmith.' As his first biographer, J.W. Mackail, explained, at the time this would not have been excused as a harmless diversion: 'a poet who chose to exercise a handicraft, not as a gentleman amateur, but under the ordinary conditions of handcraftsman, was a figure so unique as to be almost unintelligible.'

But what seemed to some a provocative statement was also the secret of Morris's

excellence both as a designer and as a shop-keeper. He never designed anything he did not know how to make himself. As an employer, he used his intimacy with materials and techniques to develop a workforce capable of realizing his ambitions; as a visionary manufacturer, he sought out craftsmen from whom to learn techniques he could then adjust to suit his needs; as an entrepreneurial decorator, he exploited his clients' amusement at his hands, a spooky blue from dyeing, or the learned tomes illustrating ancient techniques; and as a proselytizer, he wrote and lectured and demonstrated, once famously setting up his loom at an Arts and Crafts exhibition. Craft became for him the key term in an entire nexus of positive values – pleasurable physical activity, community, benign domesticity, fidelity to nature, the moral relationship between a man and his work, and, ultimately, the moral relationship between the maker and society.

Morris's expansive vision became the key inspiration of the Arts and Crafts movement, which spread throughout Europe and America from the 1880s, seeding small craft communities. In England it was perhaps C.R. Ashbee's Guild and School of Handicraft which adopted Morris's principles most faithfully, establishing a small community first in the East End of London, before moving out to Chipping Campden in the Cotswolds. Here the guild members tried to build a Utopian community, establishing craft workshops and dedicating themselves to the simple life. While some of these more earnest experiments now seem quaint and doomed to failure, their questioning of the way we live our lives and their belief in the importance of everyday objects in our lives are lasting legacies.

While Morris was a central founding figure in the various schools of thought

ABOVE LEFT: *A Morris print – Iris – and some fine craft pieces set off the clean lines of this 1930s interior as splendidly as they would a more rustic and old-fashioned home.*

ABOVE: *Edmund de Waal's ceramics are among the most beautiful and most beautifully made of their kind.*

within the modern movement in design, from Bauhaus to the studio crafts movement, his influence is still a potent force today. For Edmund de Waal, one of our leading contemporary studio potters, Morris matters because 'the compass he gave to the territory of the political life of objects and their makers still holds, it is still valid'.

At the end of it all, however, the most important thing for Morris was the creation of beautiful things. He was himself only too painfully aware of the many contradictions inherent in trying to put moral or political values at the heart of a commercial enterprise run for profit. More than that, while some of his followers, with the zeal of the converted, refused to have anything to do with industrial processes, Morris was prepared to compromise if in so doing he could make the product better, or even cheaper, and so more within the range of the artisans he so valued. Finally, craft mattered because beautiful things matter, because the most important production of art 'and the thing most to be longed for' is 'a beautiful House'. It is a belief that nobody who has ever taken pleasure in their domestic surroundings has the least trouble in identifying with. It is the impetus behind the interior design and 'house beautiful' magazines that are bought in their thousands every month, and behind the hours and hours that are spent on DIY every weekend.

BELOW: *Morris's* DAISY *design fits perfectly within this otherwise very spare and contemporary room.*

COLOUR

2

COLOUR
a distinctive palette

PERHAPS THE MOST DISTINCTIVE QUALITY of everything William Morris produced is the colour. Whether carpets or painted furniture, wallpapers or textiles, stained-glass windows or ceramic tiles, rich yet subtle colouring seems at the heart of what we think of as the 'Morris' look. As one of his most talented disciples, W.R. Lethaby, put it, 'Morris's colour-work glows from within.' But Morris's mastery over colour was not an overnight achievement. It was, rather, the sustaining quest of his life.

As a child, Morris immersed himself, precociously, in the romantic novels of Sir Walter Scott, absorbing an association between strong emotions, heroic actions and bright colours. When he was eight, his father took him to Canterbury Cathedral to see the stained-glass windows, and he felt the gates of Heaven had been opened to him. At Oxford he recognized a soul-mate in Edward Burne-Jones, who saw the days of the week as colours — Sunday was gold, Monday was yellow, and so on — and as for the Pre-Raphaelites before them, medieval colours — the deep reds and blues of the windows at Chartres, the greens of forests and village swards, the jewelled brilliance of medieval tapestries — were as central to their shared world of values as Arthurian romance. In Morris's early poetry and prose, the colours have a hallucinatory intensity and symbolic force — colours were never just colours for Morris, they were always charged with memory and emotion.

In our post-minimalist age, when we are beginning, tentatively, to allow colour back into our homes, Morris's life work shows us that colour is not just a matter of aesthetics. It is fundamental to the emotional warmth and feeling of domesticity that he saw as truly the key ingredients of the ideal home.

Indeed, as soon as Morris himself began to set up home, colour became a central factor. In their bachelor headquarters in Red Lion Square, Morris and Burne-Jones, with their friend and frequent visitor Rossetti, set about painting the extraordinary 'Barbarossa' furniture Morris had had made to his own designs. In the Red House, built for Morris on his marriage to Janey Burden by Morris's life-long friend and collaborator Philip Webb, and itself inspired by Webb's and Morris's shared love of richly coloured medieval

PREVIOUS PAGES: *This* SNAKESHEAD *furnishing fabric was designed in 1876, during a brief period in which Morris produced patterns influenced by the colouring and patterns of Indian textiles. At the same time, the rich reds and blues are quintessentially Morris, using his favourite natural dyes, indigo and madder, and recalling at once the purple of the Snakeshead fritillary, and the intense rubies and blues of medieval tapestries and stained glass.*

RIGHT: *This* HONEYSUCKLE *chintz is one of the patterns Morris designed in the mid-1870s, in the throes of his love affair with Kelmscott Manor and the surrounding countryside. It radiates pleasure in the tangled abundance of an English hedgerow in high summer.*

Camomile, Co

BIRD & ANEMONE

slip and lichen

brickwork, wall painting and embroidery were specially created to set off the building's plain but solid structure.

This collaborative effort by the loose circle of artists and friends who gathered around the Morrises directly inspired the founding of Morris, Marshall, Faulkner and Company in 1861. Setting themselves up as decorators and furniture retailers, the firm concentrated first on the skills they had so far acquired – wall painting and embroidery – but quickly added stained glass and ceramic tiles.

It was in stained glass that Morris's passion for colour first expressed itself. The revival of ritual was in full swing, and everywhere old churches were being refitted and new churches built. Morris and his associates found themselves involved in both the restoration of ancient windows and in the original design and creation of entirely new schemes. Morris oversaw, with his usual enthusiasm, every aspect of production – the design, the leading and the choice and even colouring of the glass. The groundwork of reviving the traditional skills of making stained-glass windows had already been accomplished by the first wave of neo-Gothic designers and architects, but Morris found some of their designs over-elaborate and their colours too garish. Drawing on his intimate knowledge of English fourteenth-century glass, with its muted palette of blues, rubies, yellows and greens, but also on the new colours being experimented with by the producers of stained glass, he developed a distinctive range of strong, intense colours, with white as a foil, achieving in stained glass much the same revolution in taste as he was soon to initiate in wallpaper and textiles.

Although the firm had not originally set out to produce wallpaper, by 1862 it seemed an inevitable transition. In the 1860s, wallpaper was all the rage and no decorator worth his salt could afford not to have opinions about it and several samples to hand. Once again, however, Morris's commercial antennae were matched by his perfectionism. He was determined not to compromise simply to speed up production. At first he thought to control the process through an eccentric method of etched zinc plates and oil-based inks. Eventually, however, the decision was made to print by the traditional woodblock process, a highly skilled and time-consuming hand process, but the results of which, with their pleasing irregularities and variations, are unmistakable.

With the kind of luck that Morris seemed to find in almost every sphere, where his own passionate commitment to quality found collaborators willing to experiment with him, Morris entrusted the printing of his papers to Jeffrey & Co. They had shown that the judicious mixing of modern distemper colours could produce results that were better than anything Morris could achieve. Jeffrey & Co.'s managing director from 1871, Metford Warner, was a fellow enthusiast and understood Morris's creative drive: 'tell them "not to improve my colourings" was a message I had to convey to the factory from the master in blue blouse'.

RIGHT: *This printer's log book shows the colour palette used for two of Morris's earliest wallpaper designs,* FRUIT *(or* POMEGRANATE*) and* DAISY.

Artichoke, Thistl

MorRIS & Co.

e, And Russet.

By the mid-1870s, Morris and Jeffrey & Co. had evolved a new palette – less colourful, more subtle and restrained – using pale terracottas and greeny blues. Some designs were even printed in transparent watercolour wash. Alongside this they explored dark and sombre colours, and also techniques such as embossing, metalling and lacquering, to achieve richer effects. There was no such thing as a static Morris colour scheme.

In both his wallpaper and textile design, colour and pattern evolved together. And as Morris's skills as a designer developed, so inevitably he began to demand more and more from his printers. For instance, by the end of the 1870s there were thirty-two wallpaper patterns in 125 different colourways, and whether in wallpapers or textiles, Morris was always ready to experiment with new ones: 'I can do the most ravishing yellows, rather what people call amber: what would you say to dullish pink shot with amber; like some of those chrysanthemums we see just now?' What does remain constant is an overall tone or feeling of truthfulness to the colours – they have a duskiness that recalls the colours found in nature.

And while we tend to associate Morris with an all-too-much decorative style, Morris himself deployed colour with restraint in his own homes, using monochrome walls to set off a fine tapestry or balancing the effect of flowered wallpapers and textiles with beautifully simple wooden furniture. Indeed one of the most influential innovations in the later period of Morris's reorganized business, Morris & Co., was the practice of painting walls white. White panelling was to become almost a trademark of the Arts and Crafts house, though in-keeping with Morris's preference for muted, natural colouring it was probably a rather milky white, a sort of limewash, rather than the titanium white we often see nowadays.

While Morris was developing his productive relationship with Jeffrey & Co., he was beginning an equally intense and creative relationship with another subcontractor, Thomas Wardle of Leek, Staffordshire, a printer and silk dyer. Wardle said of Morris, 'I never met a man who understood so much about colours.' Horrified by the harsh aniline dyes which, first introduced in 1857, had by the 1870s almost entirely replaced organic dyes in British textile factories, Morris had come to Wardle to see if together they could reverse this process for the dyeing of Morris & Co. textiles. He was determined to find acceptable versions of the four essential colours for the dyer – red, yellow, blue and brown – from organic sources: blue from indigo; brown from walnut roots or shells; yellow from the wild mignonette; and three types of red, from cochineal and kermes (another insect) and from the plant, madder.

Together, Wardle and Morris embarked on an obsessive quest, interrogating old dyers, reading ancient dyeing manuals, but most of all endlessly experimenting. Morris wrote to Burne-Jones' wife, Georgie, 'My days are crowded with work; not only telling unmovable Lancashire what to do, but even working in sabots and blouse in the dye house myself – you know I like that.' For three years, between 1875 and 1878, according to legend, Morris was blue from head to toe. Blue was always his favourite colour, and one of his key ambitions was to discover a reliable indigo.

ABOVE: *Here we see colours being mixed by hand for wallpaper block printing in Sanderson's wallpaper mill, the colours being matched by eye.*

RIGHT: *Morris's colour schemes were always fresh, but never harsh, and in greens and blues he favoured softer, greyer tones.*

and Fennel

Parchment, Cha

R and Manilla

Eventually Morris's and Wardle's interests began to diverge and their collaborative endeavours petered out. It was not until Morris acquired the Merton Abbey workshops in the summer of 1881, with the space and the water supply needed for dyeing, that Morris was at last able to take full control of the colour of the company's textiles. As his favourite embroiderer, Catherine Holiday, testified: 'There was a peculiar beauty in his dyeing that no one else in modern times has ever attained to. He actually did create new colours then in his amethysts and golds and greens, they were different to anything I have ever seen; he used to get a marvellous play of colour into them.' This mastery was itself an inspiration, and some of Morris's most remarkable designs for textiles are owed to these new, organic colours.

The paradox of Morris's colours, across the spectrum of his company's work, is that although they are inspired by the past, they have a wonderful freshness and originality. They trail a host of historical associations but they are also, in their subtle recall of the colours of the English countryside, deeply rooted in nature. It is this integrity and richness of resonance that gives his patterns, papers and textiles their lasting appeal.

ABOVE: *The highly effective contrast between the clean simplicity of the white room and the richly embroidered curtains is both very contemporary and echoes some of Morris's own decorative schemes, where rich fabrics, especially his beloved tapestries, were often set against white or panelled walls.*

LEFT: *This classic Morris print,* COMPTON, *complements beautifully the white painted woodwork and simple wooden floor.*

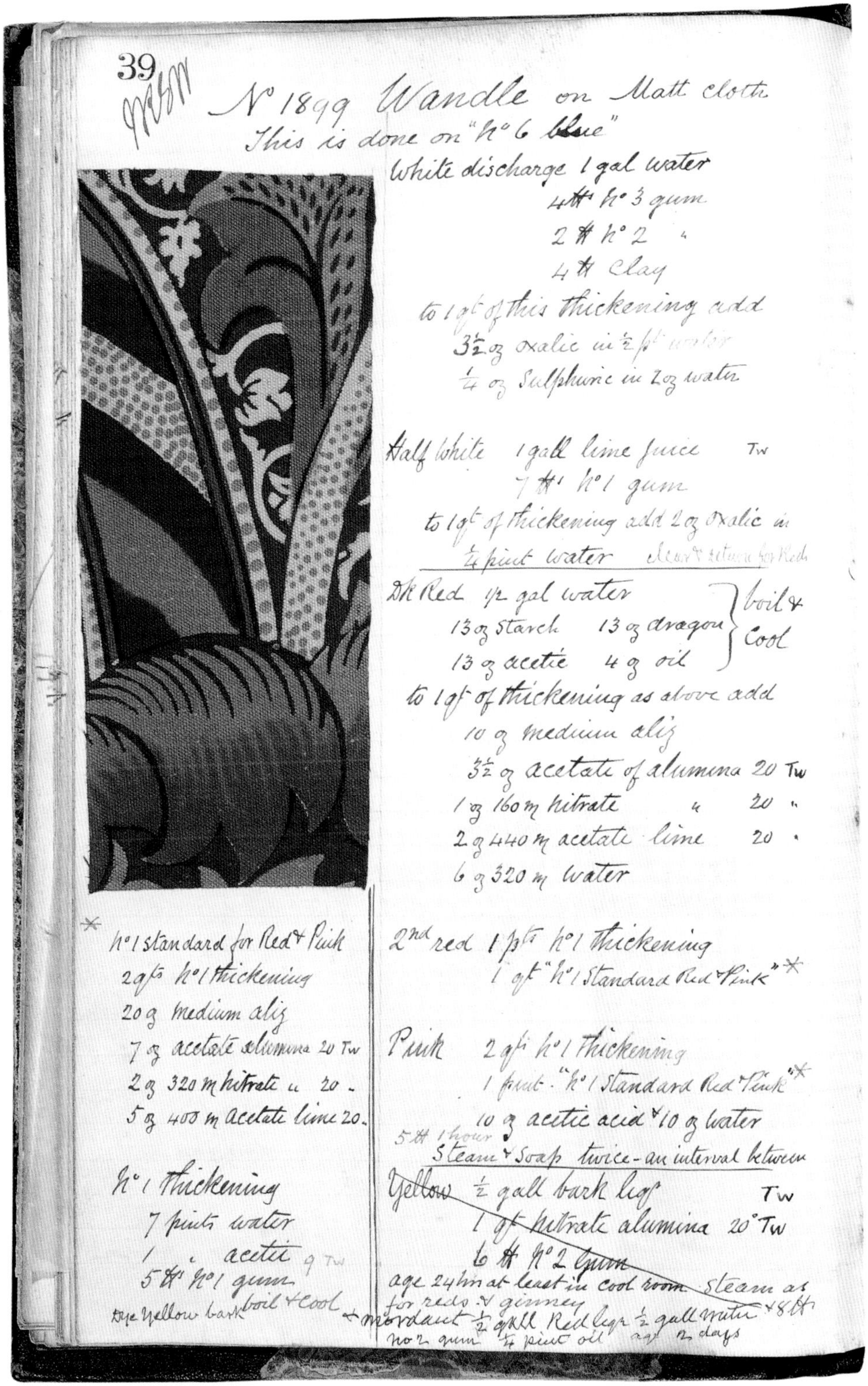

39

No 1899 Wandle on Matt cloth
This is done on "No 6 blue"

White discharge 1 gal water
4# No 3 gum
2# No 2 "
4# Clay
to 1 qt of this thickening add
3½ oz oxalic in ½ pt water
¼ oz Sulphuric in 2 oz water

Half White 1 gall lime juice Tw
7# No 1 gum
to 1 qt of thickening add 2 oz oxalic in ¼ pint water

Dk Red ½ gal water
13 oz Starch 13 oz dragon
13 oz acetic 4 oz oil
boil & Cool
to 1 qt of thickening as above add
10 oz medium aliz
3½ oz acetate of alumina 20 Tw
1 oz 160 m nitrate " 20 "
2 oz 440 m acetate lime 20 "
6 oz 320 m water

* No 1 standard for Red & Pink
2 qts No 1 thickening
20 oz medium aliz
7 oz acetate alumina 20 Tw
2 oz 320 m nitrate " 20 "
5 oz 400 m acetate lime 20

No 1 thickening
7 pints water
1 " acetic 9 Tw
5# No 1 gum
boil & cool

2nd red 1 pt No 1 thickening
1 qt "No 1 Standard Red & Pink" *

Pink 2 qts No 1 thickening
1 pint "No 1 Standard Red & Pink" *
10 oz acetic acid & 10 oz water
Steam & Soap twice - an interval between

Yellow ½ gall bark liqr Tw
1 qt nitrate alumina 20° Tw
6# No 2 Gum
age 24 hrs at least in cool room steam as for reds & ginney

RIGHT: *In 1881 Morris established his own textile factory, picturesquely located at Merton Abbey on the River Wandle. Here he was finally able to perfect the process of indigo dyeing and discharge printing. Samples of the prints produced here have been preserved in this Merton Abbey dye recipe book. Morris's enthusiasm for natural dyes is palpable in a letter to a friend: 'This morning I assisted at the dyeing of 20lbs of silk (for our damask) in the blue vat; it was very exciting, as the thing is quite unused now, and we ran a good chance of spoiling the silk. There were four dyers and Mr. Wardle at work, and myself as dyers' mate: the men were encouraged with beer and to it they went, and pretty it was to see the silk coming green out of the vat and gradually turning blue: we succeeded very well as far as we can tell at present.'*

Indigo, Slate

MORRIS & CO.

e and Ivory

HONESTY

3

HONESTY
no excess, fakery or pastiche

I N JANUARY 1861 DANTE GABRIEL ROSSETTI WROTE to his friend William Allingham announcing the imminent birth of Morris, Marshall, Faulkner and Company: 'We are not intending to compete with Crace's costly rubbish or anything of that sort, but to give real good taste at the price if possible of ordinary furniture...' Many a manufacturer since has claimed to be trying to make the best possible and to charge only what he really needed to, but few have tried as hard as Morris to deliver on this promise. The commitment to 'real good taste' was a moral crusade, and the effort to charge at least an honest, if not, to Morris's dismay, ever a modest price, was a founding principle.

Honesty was, perhaps, the central virtue uniting Morris's activities on every front. His fundamental integrity as a person is refracted differently through each preoccupation and explains his continuing appeal today. You may not agree with his politics or share his romantic idealization of the medieval era, but his restless pursuit of the true principles underlying every branch of the decorative arts was undeniably admirable, and his commitment to quality – good materials, honest workmanship and high aesthetic values – has ensured that his designs have endured.

When Morris and his friends set up their first commercial company they were fired with the ambition, inspired by John Ruskin, to fight what they saw as the degraded taste of their time. Among their competitors was the fashionable firm of J.G. Crace, decorator to the aristocracy, whose High Renaissance suite of rooms at Windsor Castle in particular represented a servile historicism and rampant luxury they despised.

Morris's pronouncements on furniture summed up the firm's principles: 'our furniture should be good citizen's furniture, solid and well made in workmanship, and in design should have nothing about it that is not easily defensible, no monstrosities or extravagances, not even of beauty, lest we weary of it'. This did not mean that you could not have beautiful and even elaborate pieces. Morris

PREVIOUS PAGES: *This* SUNFLOWER *design may be derived from nature but celebrates its two-dimensional status as pure pattern rather than attempting to create an illusion. The pattern is utterly straightforward, with no attempt to disguise the obvious horizontal and vertical repeats, and there is no pattern in the background to distract attention from the main design.*

ABOVE: *The interior of Red House, designed by Philip Webb, speaks of solidity and simplicity. The naked wood, plain brick and white walls make the architecture explicit, and create a space that is suffused with light and easily lived in.*

BELOW: *There is a timeless quality about Red House that derives from the harmony and integrity of its design. The German critic Hermann Muthesius commented in 1904 that it was the first house 'to be conceived and built as a unified whole, inside and out, the very first in the history of the modern house'. In turn it came to influence not only the design of English Arts and Crafts houses, but also the international modernist school.*

distinguished between 'necessary work-a-day furniture' and 'state furniture', and positively encouraged the use of carving, inlaying and painting in the latter. But all pieces were to be made 'of timber rather than walking sticks' and according to 'the proper principles of the art of joinery'. His only designs for furniture, for his own rooms, fulfilled these precepts to the letter. Huge, heavy and, as Rossetti described them, 'intensely medieval', these tables and chairs 'like incubi and succubi…such as Barbarossa might have sat on', might today seem merely quaint and eccentric, but at the time they represented a defiant protest in favour of substance and the evidently hand-made, and against the genteel refinements of contemporary taste.

The same values are at work in Morris's fabrics and wallpapers, his stained glass and ceramics, his carpets and tapestries. These also show the benefits of his determination to grasp — in the full sense of that word — the principles that underlie

each production process. His championship of the low tech, his effort to master the different craft technologies himself, his pursuit of natural dyes and beautiful yarns, his scholar's zeal in amassing a vast collection of historical examples of each craft, which he then studied minutely, point to his constant tactile engagement with the realities of his business.

Morris shared with the Pre-Raphaelite Brotherhood of painters a moral emphasis on drawing from life as the lifeblood of art and craft. The source of all true inspiration is nature itself, and drawing from life is the only defence against cliché and pastiche. Combined with Ruskin's poetic picture of the Gothic craftsman, lovingly attentive to every detail of the natural and human world he is trying to depict, Morris found himself committed to weeks of preparatory sketching and research

BELOW: Morris designs can be used in multifarious ways – they can be used in the simplest and most unpretentious ways, but can also contribute to more formal settings.

RIGHT: *The round dining table at Kelmscott Manor sums up the spirit of fellowship, hospitality and warmth that Morris felt were essential to a real home.*

ABOVE: *This battered Sussex chair, from the range produced by Morris & Co. from 1866 onwards, looks perfectly at home alongside the original exposed 16th-century panels in Kelmscott Manor.*

before he dared draw a flower or a bird. This is what gives his patterns their distinctive charm – they ring true to the nature they evoke.

Morris was at the forefront of the fight against fakery, challenging a number of the leading neo-Gothic designers and architects who were busy restoring old churches up and down the land in accordance with their own notions of how a Gothic church should look. Ruskin's anathema on restoration: '[it] means the most total destruction, a destruction out of which no remnants can be gathered, a destruction accompanied with false description of the thing destroyed' was a call to arms, and Morris responded in 1877 by helping to found the famous organization SPAB (the Society

LEFT: *This simple reproduction Morris tile is a homely grace note in this otherwise rather austere setting.*

BELOW: *The drawing room at Kelmscott House would have looked very plain to Victorian eyes. The patterned hangings (BIRD), table cloth and carpets in no way smother but in fact enhance beautifully the elegant simplicity of the room, with its matching cabinets and symmetrical arrangement of bowls and furniture.*

RIGHT: *It was a basic tenet held by Ruskin, Pugin, Morris and others that honesty in design demanded that you did not try to create a three-dimensional illusion in a two-dimensional design. Wallpaper should not disguise the flatness of the surface but enhance it. This GARDEN TULIP design shows very shallow relief effects, with little shading and a limited palette, but this enhances rather than detracts from the pattern's strength.*

ABOVE: *Morris with Jenny and May by Edward Burne-Jones. Far from the remote Victorian father of legend, Morris loved family life and played a large part in bringing up his two daughters.*

for the Protection of Ancient Buildings). Although Morris had himself learned much about ancient buildings through his brief spell working on their restoration under the architect G.E. Street, he now developed a particularly impressive line in fiery invective against what he identified as misguided attempts to tidy up the past.

Powerful as Morris's influence has been in the conservation of ancient religious and public buildings, his most original legacy has been in his vision of how to create a home, a truly domestic space. Here it is his insistence on simplicity, his ability to balance the ornate and the spare, and his unerring instinct for genuine beauty that particularly inspired his contemporaries and is still inspiring today. As George Bernard Shaw remarked about Kelmscott House in Hammersmith, it was the sparseness of decoration that was so startling in a Morris house: 'On the supper table there was no table cloth: a thing common enough now among people who see that a table should be itself an ornament and not a clothes horse, but then an innovation so staggering that it cost years of domestic conflict to introduce it.' The Arts and Crafts house, with its love of simple decoration but emphasis on space, light and air, is a physical manifestation of an entire ethos that values nature above artifice, the genuine above the unreal, the open and transparent above the enclosed and over-complicated. And in the end, Morris's emphasis is not aesthetic at all: 'It is not an original remark, but I make it here, that my home is where I meet people with whom I sympathise, whom I love.' It is this instinct for warmth, homeliness and fellowship, and how these can be fostered by decoration, that was his real gift.

It was those human qualities too that he argued needed to underlie the making of decorative art, if it was to be any good. In saying, as he did so many times in his lectures, that 'that thing which I understand by real art is the expression by man of his pleasure in labour', Morris was unequivocally rooting aesthetic value in the social and economic circumstances of the craftsman. He believed that beautiful wallpaper required honest relations between a manufacturer and his workers, a pleasant and

BELOW: *This interior evokes the simple, clean look of a Morris house, full of life but uncluttered.*

LEFT: *This dining room, in a modern American home, exemplifies the American take on Morris, where Morris's values sit easily alongside homegrown Shaker principles. Here, the dining room is the warm heart of the house. The table is not fussily over-dressed, but looks ready for use at any moment.*

sociable working environment, a decent wage and a degree of autonomy and respect for the individual craftsman. He was also only too aware of how often his own business fell short of these ideals.

Moreover, far from fulfilling Rossetti's proud boast that their furnishings would cost no more than ordinary furniture, Morris's insistence on the best materials and the most labour-intensive technologies took the price of most of his products way beyond the reach of his model artisan.

Instead of shrugging his shoulders at this conflict between his hopes and the economic realities of high Victorian capitalism, between his private values and his

RIGHT: *Morris's stylized designs are equally at home in Japan. In this schoolhouse the simple exposed structure and bare walls are balanced by panels of richly decorative sliding screens. Morris's* BIRD AND ANEMONE *fabric provides a focused area of colour and ornament in an otherwise clean, unadorned space.*

professional need to make his business a going concern, Morris became a revolutionary socialist. In this way he lived out the contradictions inherent in his dual identity as capitalist and communist visionary, which is itself a kind of honesty. And although during the period when he was most involved with political campaigning he confessed, 'Poetry goes with the hand-arts I think, and like them has now become unreal', he did not abandon either his pattern-work or his writing.

In our ideologically more chastened times, we should be grateful for that. For it is in the substance of his wallpapers, fabrics, carpets and embroideries that his own finest qualities of warmth, imagination and integrity persist.

LEFT AND ABOVE: *In the completely different setting of an urban home, Morris paint and fabrics can be used to create a wonderfully simple, unadorned effect.*

PATTERN

4

PATTERN
his great talent

WILLIAM MORRIS WAS A PATTERN-MAKER of genius. W.R. Lethaby called him 'the greatest pattern-designer we ever had or ever can have'. Morris discovered his bent in the summer vacation of 1857, when, recruited by Dante Gabriel Rossetti to paint Arthurian murals in the Oxford Union, he had insuperable difficulties with the figures. He was sent to find a model to work from:

> *Poor Topsy has gone to make a sketch of Miss Lipscombe*
> *But he can't draw the head, and don't know where the hips come.*

Miss Lipscombe not obliging, Morris threw himself into painting a huge, complicated mythological design with repeats, covering the roof – and discovered a passion for pattern that was to last his lifetime.

Morris brought to pattern the ardour and moral energy he invested in all his activities. While patterns had to be beautiful – if they were not, he urged people to do without pattern altogether and paint their walls white – they should also draw out the meaning of the buildings they adorned. They should soothe the spirit and point to life beyond themselves: 'You may be sure that any decoration is futile, and has fallen into at least the first stage of degradation, when it does not remind you of something beyond itself, of something of which it is but a visible symbol.' We may not be used to articulating our thoughts about design in quite these elevated terms, but Morris's seriousness of purpose is a key to the lasting appeal of his patterns and to their ability to knit themselves into our lives.

His first three patterns, produced for wallpapers in 1864, draw together reminiscence, suggestion and pure aesthetic pleasure in a way that set the standard for everything to come. *Daisy* was inspired by the clump-of-flowers motif Morris had discovered in a medieval French manuscript in the British Museum. He had set his wife Janey to embroidering it on a piece of blue serge as one of the first textiles for Red House, but the pattern was to prove lastingly popular both as a wallpaper and for embroidery. *Trellis* was directly inspired by Red House, and by Morris's and Philip

52

Webb's attempts to create the perfect domestic environment. Based on the rose trellises around the central courtyard, it evokes a middle ground between house and garden, between the order of the trained, though ominously barbed, rose bushes and the free flight of the humming birds. Although Morris was later to invest a great deal of time in learning how to draw birds and animals for his designs, these birds were drawn by Philip Webb – an example of the friendly collaboration which was so much part of the spirit of Morris, Marshall, Faulkner and Company. The third paper – *Fruit* (or *Pomegranate*) – evokes a mythological world of pleasure and temptation, and

BELOW: *Most of Morris's designs sprang from his direct experience of the nature that surrounded him – in this case, the willow trees that lined the banks of a stream that flowed into the Thames.*

RIGHT: *This* ARTICHOKE *hanging was designed by Morris in 1877 and was worked by Mrs Godman for her Philip Webb-designed house. The pattern – using large traditional motifs – was perhaps inspired by Near Eastern and Italian woven fabrics seen by Morris at the South Kensington Museum, now the V&A.*

in its free-flowing diagonal movement (Morris argued that 'the continuous line' in decoration was the great contribution of the Byzantine world to Western culture) shows how easily Morris wore his exhaustive knowledge of the history of pattern-making.

These papers, while more stiffly formal than Morris's wonderful patterns of the 1870s and 1880s, make clear Morris's originality – his fresh observation of nature, his sense of humour, his strong draughtsmanship, his insistence on 'rational growth' in pattern, in which every element 'grows visibly and necessarily from another', but also his instinct for freedom and exuberance within the demands of the repeating pattern. Morris marked out a territory between the overly naturalistic, sentimental French chintzes then popular and the sternly geometric designs of the English 'reformed' school of Owen Jones, that still holds good today. As his latest biographer, Fiona MacCarthy, has beautifully said: 'He found in art and nature the sources of

ABOVE: *The gardens at Red House were a direct inspiration for many of Morris's early designs. If a formal garden brings order into nature, Morris's designs in turn bring nature back into the home.*

LEFT: TRELLIS *was Morris's first wallpaper design. Morris always loved these early, simple patterns, and hung a blue-ground version of* TRELLIS *in his bedroom at Kelmscott House. As his first biographer, J.W. Mackail, pointed out, it recalls the 'wattled rose-trellises enclosing richly-flowered square garden plots' at Red House.*

resilience. I think his patterns have lasted on right through another century because they still convey to us a little of that hope.'

But Morris was not just a pattern-designer. He was a pattern-maker and a decorator, with very definite views not only on which patterns were appropriate for which materials and techniques – his designs for printed and woven textiles, wallpapers and carpets are all quite different – but also on how patterns should be used to decorate a home.

Far from the clichéd image of dark rooms crowded with patterned papers and fabric, Morris's own homes were famously simple and beautiful. He believed that only one patterned paper should be used in a room and, fighting the Victorian tendency to divide the wall into sections, all calling for different treatments, sometimes ran a single paper from the skirting to the ceiling. He disliked papered ceilings – 'a room papered all over would be like a box to live in' – and would equally

RIGHT: *The original design for* ACANTHUS *wallpaper. Dating from 1874, this was the first of a group of large-scale, heavily patterned and dark-coloured papers. Morris used fifteen subtly different colours – more than in any previous design (and a headache for the printers) – but this, together with the bold, sinuous marking of the leaves, is the secret of the pattern's vigour.*

ABOVE: *The dining room of 7 Hammersmith Terrace shows an exemplary Arts and Crafts use of pattern, undogmatically mixing and matching old and new in a layered but still remarkably uncluttered look. The uncovered wooden table, the simple ladder-back chair and the plain white ceiling provide points of calm for the eye, around which the rest of the ensemble can cohere.*

LEFT: *If the previous picture shows us how a contemporary of Morris made use of his patterns, opera director Lindsay Kemp's house in Umbria shows us that Morris's designs can be used just as vibrantly today. Here, Kemp combines Morris's paper (FRUIT (or POMEGRANATE)) with a variety of ethnic textiles to give his apartment a thoroughly modern, slightly Boho air.*

have abhorred the claustrophobic effect of matching curtains to wallpaper to bedroom linen, and so on.

It wasn't that he objected to richness of effect – his particular passion was for often richly decorated textile hangings, whether embroidered, woven or printed, hung the whole length of the wall – but that this needed to be offset by plain wooden or painted furniture, panelled or painted walls, or by a plain wooden floor. While this balancing of pattern with plainness harks back to Morris's beloved medieval era, it also resonates strongly with our highly contemporary eclecticism, where the dogma of minimalism has been broken down to allow a much freer mix and match. As a number of contemporary interiors testify, you can use Morris's patterns sparely or layer upon layer, as a single subtle note or flamboyantly juxtaposed, to achieve a whole range of different effects and to suit a variety of different rooms.

Above all, Morris saw the decorative scheme, both of his own and other people's

BELOW: *The library at Wightwick Manor shows a similarly relaxed attitude to mixing patterns, without fussing too much about whether or not they match.*

LEFT: *Morris's muted* PINK AND ROSE *design is matched with some generously contrasting fabrics to create a comfortable, informal retreat.*

RIGHT: *Lindsay Kemp's bedroom in his Umbrian farmhouse again uses Morris paints and fabrics alongside ethnic carpets and antique furniture to create a warm but contemporary and entirely idiosyncratic interior.*

houses, as a whole, and he made a clear distinction between the kind of patterns appropriate for a town house and those appropriate for a country house. In fact his vision was so all-inclusive that no detail was exempt, and the garden or surrounding cityscape was as much an active component in the overall effect as a specific wallpaper or carpet. For one client, for instance, he created a luxurious though conventionally fashionable London home, abundant in specially designed ceiling and wall decoration, furniture and carpets. In their country house he used light-coloured woods, plain colours, machine-woven carpeting and printed cottons, anticipating much Arts and Crafts decoration.

That he could turn his hand – and indeed his patterns – to either commission, however, is the real testimony to the range and versatility of his designs. In his lifetime Morris was responsible for approximately seventy patterns, about fifty of them his own work. This is a tiny output compared with any major manufacturer. They have, however, had an influence that far exceeds their number, an influence based on the ebullience of their evocations of nature and their rich, formal complexity. As his disciple Lethaby said, Morris's patterns are not merely delights, 'they are depths', and these depths still resonate for us today.

BELOW RIGHT: *Because Morris's patterns draw so richly on nature, even the most elaborate and highly coloured have a freshness and simplicity that comes from direct observation.*

LEFT: *This interior shows how effective a restrained use of Morris pattern can be in a room otherwise kept remarkably simple. The rich colouring of the* GOLDEN LILY *paper and the brightness of the* IRIS *cushion fabric bring warmth and character to what might otherwise seem a rather cool and spartan interior, without destroying the overall mood of simplicity and naturalness conveyed by wood, stone and rush.*

NATURE

NATURE
a source of inspiration

In *The Lesser Arts of Life* (1882), Morris wrote: 'Lastly, love of nature in all its forms must be the ruling spirit of such works of art as we are considering.' This was undoubtedly true for Morris himself. He had adopted the idea, as a critical principle, from Ruskin's lyrical hymn to medieval craftsmen, 'On the Nature of Gothic', but as the driving energy in his own design work, and the key to its vitality, this love was embedded deeply in his own nature.

In the most obvious sense, almost every pattern he ever created – whether for wallpaper, textiles, stained-glass windows, or for the beautiful Kelmscott Press initial letters and borders – had a flower or plant motif. Animals, birds and butterflies creep, hop and flutter through his work. More generally, the freedom he took with design conventions – the complex layering of effects, the intricate intertwinings of branches and tendrils, his daring extension of the area of a design before it is repeated – was inspired by an emulative love of nature's own richness and exuberance.

From childhood he responded intensely to landscape – the flat, marshy Essex countryside he explored on his Shetland pony, and Epping Forest, dense and mysterious with hornbeams and holly thickets. Later, as a schoolboy at Marlborough College, he added the water meadows of Wiltshire, the sweeping Marlborough Downs and medieval Savernake Forest to his catalogue of treasured places. Wherever he travelled – Northern France, Iceland, Bad Ems in Central Germany – his letters are full of observations about landscape, and his poetry and prose are alight with the heraldic brightness of birds, flowers and animals. His excitement seems always to have been partly a direct sensuous response to landscape, and to the plants, birds and beasts that inhabit it, and partly a vivid imaginative engagement with the human histories embedded there.

Morris combined the spirit of the romantic, alive to the numinous power of rivers and woods and able to see eternity in a flower, with the precise eye of the botanist or zoologist. He was, after all, a contemporary of both the Pre-Raphaelites and of Charles Darwin. Though he felt good draughtsmanship and an accurate eye

PREVIOUS PAGES: *The* STRAWBERRY THIEF *textile was derived directly from a moment when Morris saw some thrushes creeping under the strawberry nets in the garden at Kelmscott. This design called upon Morris's newly perfected indigo-discharge dyeing technique.*

RIGHT: *The* PIMPERNEL *wallpaper, with its small, intensely blue flowerheads, was used by Morris to decorate his dining room at Kelmscott House. The contrast between the controlled formality of the pattern's mirror symmetry and the wild, almost windblown vitality of the large white flowerheads, is typical of Morris's greatest designs.*

ABOVE: *This cushion, covered in the Morris fabric* IRIS, *blends as easily into its surroundings on a rough bench in the garden as it would in a formal drawing room.*

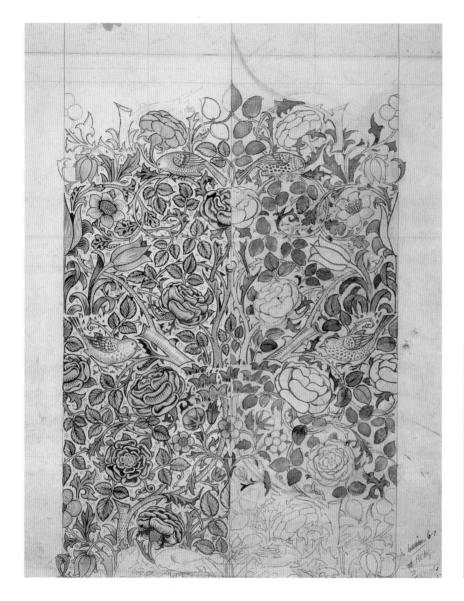

CHRYSANTHEMUM	10 - 11 -	Illustrated
APPLE	3 9	,,
BOWER	9	
MALLOW	3 9 to 5 -	Design Miss Faulkner
*SUNFLOWER	4 6 6 -	Illustrated
*ACORN	4 6 5 -	
BRAMBLE	7 6 8 6	Design Miss Faulkner
*POPPY	4 6 to 5 3	With gold 21 -
*ST. JAMES'S	32 6	Designed for St. James's Palace
*BIRD AND ANEMONE	4 - 5 -	
HONEYSUCKLE	8 6	Design Miss Morris
*CHRISTCHURCH	5 - 5 9	
*GRAFTON	4 6	
*WILD TULIP	8 6	With gold 25 -
BLOSSOM	9 6	Design Miss Faulkner
HORN POPPY	5 - to 6 -	Design Miss Morris
*FRITILLARY	5 - to 5 9	
*GARDEN TULIP	8 6 8 8	
*LILY AND POMEGRANATE	12 6	Illustrated

were the key to all good design, he despised what he referred to as 'sham naturalistic platitude'. At the other extreme, however, he also shied away from the exquisite but rather static formalism of Augustus Pugin and others of the Gothic revival. He saw his own art in organic terms as 'alive, growing, and looking toward the future'; it was part of the nature it was trying to express, and that dynamism can be felt clearly in his designs.

Nature and culture were thus always inextricably intertwined for him – and it is this that gives his patterns their enduring power. The freshness of direct observation is given depth and resonance by Morris's use of colour and his sure sense of structure, both of which evoke the whole history of man's creative response to nature. Yet

RIGHT: *The* WILD TULIP *wallpaper design shows how skilfully Morris could capture the simplicity of a country garden in a pattern that in fact uses many subtly different colours and required eighteen printing blocks to complete it.*

ABOVE: *A late design,* BLACKTHORN *dates from 1892 and, with its dark, leafy background and bright woodland flowers, evokes tangled English woodland with an almost Pre-Raphaelite intensity.*

Morris's designs are not fustily indebted to the past: they are infused with the spirit of the English garden and hedgerow. As May Morris, Morris's younger daughter, remarked in 1936 of her father's 1884 design *Wild Tulip*: 'The character of this design is all Kelmscott to me: the peony and wild tulip are two of the richest blossomings of the spring garden at the Manor...' It is as if the Kelmscott spring is happening all over again.

Nature worked in Morris as a direct inspiration. He seized on what he found around him: 'those natural forms which are at once most familiar and most delightful to us, as well from association as from beauty, are the best for our purpose. The rose, the lily, the tulip, the oak, the vine, and all the herbs and trees that even we cockneys know about…' The trellis in the garden at Red House prompted one of his earliest wallpaper patterns, *Trellis*. The orchard of apple trees and cherry trees; the white jasmine, roses, honeysuckle and passion flower trained up the red-brick walls; the lilies and sunflowers in the garden, all find their echo in his work. Later, it was Kelmscott Manor, Morris's country home between 1871 and 1896, and the surrounding countryside that inspired his surge of activity in the 1870s. The William Morris chintzes, *Honeysuckle, Tulip, Marigold, Iris, Carnation*, and wallpapers such as *Larkspur* and *Chrysanthemum*, all owe their ebullience to this new love. Finally, perhaps the high point of his achievement in textile design, the series of patterns based on the tributaries of the Thames – *Windrush, Evenlode, Kennet, Wey, Wandle* and *Medway* – owe their poetic beauty to Morris's lifelong love affair with rivers, and above all the Thames.

More indirectly, Morris's mission to revive the art of dyeing using traditional vegetable dyes was born from an instinct that if you were to paint nature true you should use nature's own colours. Eccentric as this opinion might have seemed in the nineteenth century, heyday of industrial positivism, it makes another sense today when we are only too aware of the poisonous consequences of chemical dyes for our rivers and streams.

Beyond his work as a designer, Morris the architect and decorator took as much interest in gardens as in houses, endeavouring, as he achieved with Philip Webb at Red House, to bring the garden into as close a relationship with the house as possible, opening windows and doors out onto the garden and using his fabrics and papers to bring the garden into the house. Morris expressed his view on the garden in the lecture 'Making the Best of It' in 1879: 'large and small, it should look both orderly and rich. It should be well fenced from the outside world. It should by no means imitate either

BELOW: *Standen House and gardens in West Sussex. Standen House was designed by Philip Webb, who, on principle, employed local craftsmen and local materials in its building. The house thus grows very much out of the landscape, both natural and human, achieving for a new house the sense of belonging that usually requires centuries to acquire.*

the wilfulness or wildness of nature, but should look like a thing never to be seen except near a house. It should in fact look like part of the house.' This embracing of nature became a guiding principle in all Arts and Crafts buildings, leading architects to create light and airy spaces opening onto gardens where the Victorians had preferred to immure themselves in sequences of dark and over-decorated rooms.

As a visionary and idealist, Morris extrapolated his belief in the benign influence of nature to propose that all people should live in rural communities, modelled on the still medieval patterning of villages he loved so much in Oxfordshire around Kelmscott Manor, with no-one more than five minutes from open countryside. In this environment everyone's wants would be few and 'I think one might hope civilisation had really begun'. This ideal has been the inspiration for rural Arts and Crafts communities still found today throughout Europe and America, and had a profound impact on the creation of garden cities.

Much as Morris's thinking about nature pointed to the future, however, it was also shot through with a pervasive nostalgia and sense of imminent threat. He was

RIGHT: *When Morris stumbled upon Kelmscott Manor he wrote ecstatically of it to his old friend Charles Faulkner: 'a heaven on earth; an old stone Elizabethan house like Water Eaton, and such a garden! close down on the river, a boat house and all things handy.' It combined all his loves – the 'beautiful and strangely naïf house' itself, the romantic garden and the River Thames, with its wide river meadows, which Morris had known since a boy in East London.*

LEFT: *Kelmscott Manor embodied all Morris's ideals of a building so naturally part of its environment that it was as if it had 'grown up out of the soil and the lives of them that lived on it'. He had seen it in a dream before he discovered it in reality in 1871.*

LEFT: *An interior at Kelmscott House, where Morris used* KENNET *fabric to remind us, inside, of the river flowing nearby. The* KENNET *textile pattern, named after a tributary of the Thames, was one of a series directly inspired by Morris's love of the River Thames. It evokes in its wavy, diagonal patterning the movement of the river, while also summoning the flowers and plants you would find along its edges.*

acutely aware of the damage that industrial processes and urban development were doing to nature. This feeling for the precious vulnerability of nature surfaces in his design work as a cherishing attention to all the minute particulars of flowers and birds. As a political activist it led Morris to devote his later years to preserving the countryside through his involvement with such groups as the Kyrle Society, a forerunner of the National Trust. One of his last public campaigns was an attempt to halt the felling of his beloved hornbeam trees in Epping Forest. An eco-warrior of his time, it is a measure of his integrity as a person and the far reach of his vision that he should at the end have sought to preserve the source of all his inspiration and solace for future generations.

ABOVE: *The Hayes' cottage in a wood, a modern American take on the Arts and Crafts aesthetic, looks as if it has grown there, its own walls and windows echoing and reflecting the dappled pattern of trees and sunlight in the garden.*

LEFT: *This open door to the Hayes' cottage, with its Morris pattern on the wall inside and the climbing rose peeping in, exemplifies the Arts and Crafts understanding of how house and garden should be one continuous whole, inside and outside flowing together, echoing each other.*

ABOVE: *While Morris loved formal gardens – the plots and trellises of Red House, for instance – that did not mean that nature had to be too tidy or tamed. Here, the weeds are creeping back through the stone and reclaiming the bench.*

LEGEND

6

LEGEND
combining old and new

IN SOME LINEAGES OF MODERN DESIGN, William Morris is placed at the top, a bearded patriarch, fierce in his denunciation of the false flummery of much Victorian decoration, one of the ideological forefathers of modernism. He famously said, 'Have nothing in your houses that you do not know to be useful, or believe to be beautiful', and so is much honoured by those who see function as the source of all beauty in furniture and decoration. In fact, he himself believed that the beautiful mattered greatly, even defending such superfluous pleasures as eccentrically neo-Gothic painted furniture or highly patterned curtains, and he had a predilection for decoration that was resonant with both romance and history.

One of the dreams of modernism, that global movement in art, design and architecture that dominated the twentieth century, was that you could produce architecture and design that were free of associations, cut loose from the past, redeemed from the values and attitudes of our ancestors. In spare white rooms with metal, plastic or glass furnishings that barely show the signs of age, you could be truly free to be who you wanted to be. Of course, this was an illusion. We all carry our own past and the cultural baggage of our times around with us, bound to us as intimately as a snail's shell, and those white spaces were soon filled with photographs and books, paintings and sculptures, heirlooms, gifts and mementoes. In time, the white space itself and the furniture that went with it became ancestral in their own right, weighty with meaning.

Today we require that our furniture and decoration, far from aspiring to the condition of blankness, speak to us openly of our hopes and desires, our dreams and our memories. Morris himself was quite explicit. Speaking of patterns, he wrote:

> *I, as a Western man and a picture-lover, must still insist on plenty of meaning in your patterns; I must have unmistakable suggestions of gardens and fields, and strange trees, boughs, and tendrils, or I can't do with your pattern, but must take the first piece of nonsense-work a Kurdish shepherd has woven from tradition and memory; all the more, as even in that there will be some hint of past history.*

ABOVE: *The rooms at Wightwick Manor evoke romance and legend. Each item is rich in meaning, but all is tempered by comfortable practicality.*

RIGHT: *Morris's fabrics, built up layer on layer, are intrinsic to the evocation of a romantic, pseudo-medieval atmosphere at Wightwick Manor.*

In his own houses, from Red House to Kelmscott, however sparsely furnished his rooms, the wallpaper and textiles, the furniture and carpets, together evoked the richly blended world of legend and history where Morris was spiritually most at home. Plain English furniture – a Jacobean table, a medieval bench – would be enhanced by an elaborate hand-woven hanging or hand-knotted carpet; a beautiful piece of furniture, painted with figures, would be set against a plain white wall. What Morris once said about medieval tapestry weaving could stand for all the decorative arts:

> *To turn our chamber walls into the green woods of the leafy month of June, populous of bird and beast; or a summer garden with man and maid playing round a fountain, or a solemn procession of the mythical warriors and heroes of old; that surely was worth the trouble of doing, and the money that had to be paid for it: that was no languid acquiescence in an upholsterer's fashion.*

LEFT: *Janey Morris's chance discovery of a piece of indigo-dyed blue serge in a London shop inspired Morris to design the DAISY pattern for her to embroider onto it. Uniting his love of indigo with his passion for simple medieval motifs, this homemade cloth hanging is a quintessential piece of Morris interior decoration.*

ABOVE: *The* CRAY *fabric of the curtains, set against the same design as a wallpaper, helps create a lushly romantic look. This complicated pattern, designed in the 1880s, became one of the company's most popular designs.*

RIGHT: *As a wallpaper, the* CRAY *design looks almost as though it were hand-painted onto the wall, evoking faded medieval frescoes.*

LEFT: *This* BIRD AND ANEMONE *design, which was used for both wallpapers and textiles, simultaneously evokes the natural world outside the window and the legendary world, quasi-medieval, quasi-oriental, which had such a powerful hold on Morris's imagination from his childhood. It resonates beautifully with the simple antique furniture in this room.*

RIGHT: *Fabrics could act as pathways into other realms of the imagination, both legendary and historic, as illustrated in this detail from Kelmscott Manor.*

ABOVE: *We tend to think that Morris the designer was exclusively inspired by nature. Just as important to him was literature, and the kinds of romantic depiction of nature that he found in poetry as much as in illuminated manuscripts and historic textiles.*

As this makes clear, even nature comes laden with cultural associations and emotional memories. Whether he was painting a narrative scene on a wardrobe or designing a pattern with animals and flowers, fables and legends, and the mythic medieval England he wove from history, Sir Thomas Malory's *Le Morte D'Arthur* and Chaucer, were as important sources of inspiration as the birds, trees and flowers themselves.

The association between decoration and story-telling was rooted deeply in Morris's childhood. In *The Lesser Arts of Life*, he remembers as a boy first coming upon a room hung with faded medieval tapestries...

... at Queen Elizabeth's Lodge, by Chingford Hatch, in Epping Forest (I wonder what has become of it now), and the impression of romance that it made upon me; a feeling that always comes back on me when I read, as I often do, Sir Walter Scott's Antiquary, and come to the

description of the green room at Monkbarns, amongst which the novelist has with such exquisite cunning of art imbedded the fresh and glittering verses of the summer poet Chaucer; yes, that was more than upholstery, believe me.

It is hard to tell where decoration ends and literature begins. To those who think of Morris primarily in the context of design, it is a reminder that he was, in fact, first of all a poet, a creator of legends, and most famous among his contemporaries not for being the designer of the *Strawberry Thief* but for being the author of *The Earthly Paradise.* His poems and novels were intensely romantic, set either in a mythic past or a visionary future, and written in a sing-song rhythm like ancient sagas. His dedication to legend is evident, too, not just in the literary works he translated — especially the Icelandic sagas, but also *Beowulf,* Homer's *Odyssey* and *The Aeneid* of Virgil — but also in the books he chose to publish at the Kelmscott Press. Here, his design — the beautiful borders and initial letters as well as the different typefaces he discovered — sprang immediately from literature.

The twin worlds of legend and medieval England were not just sources of imagery for Morris. They were a moral inspiration. At Oxford, Morris and Burne-Jones had entered wholeheartedly into the Victorian cult of Arthurian legend, then approaching its grand climax. They adopted the chivalric code not as a picturesque

ABOVE: *This famous picture of the ghostly Morris in his study at Kelmscott House reminds us that he was known to his contemporaries first and foremost as a writer and a poet. As May Morris, his younger daughter, remembered it, his study was 'almost frugally bare', with no carpets or curtains and a plain deal board on trestles as a writing table. It was furnished with books. Morris was a writer, translator, calligrapher and collector of ancient books. He also made books as the printer and publisher of the Kelmscott Press.*

ABOVE: *These stained-glass quarries, designed by Philip Webb for Red House, are inspired by medieval black and yellow stained glass and reflect Morris's love of heraldic or fabulous plants and creatures.*

RIGHT: *One of the panels of the months and signs of the zodiac painted by Burne-Jones in 1866 for the Green Dining Room in the South Kensington Museum. This was a substantial official commission for Morris's company, and drew on their reputation as decorators able to provide details that were instructive and inspiring, but that should also constitute works of art in themselves.*

LEFT AND BELOW: *Although Morris's patterns are richly allusive – to nature, to history and to legend – they are not inflexibly tied to one style or period of decoration. They work as easily alongside modern furniture and architecture as in period settings. Indeed, they are almost happiest in this kind of Bohemian setting, where pieces from many different eras rub harmoniously along together. After all, this was the kind of eclectic mix of decoration and furniture that Morris himself preferred.*

affectation but as a religious and ethical guide to life, and the theme of the search for the Holy Grail preoccupied them both throughout their lives.

Nor was this simply a dreamy nostalgia. Morris could not bear pastiche and fought a lifelong campaign against it, whether in architecture, literature or design. What Morris wanted to discover was a living tradition of art and morality on a par in its strength and authenticity with the medieval tradition, but not slavishly imitative of any one element in it. This explains the indelible modernity in his figures and the modern sensibility at work in his patterns. His designs were not meant simply to recover a past, nor solely to speak to his own age, but perhaps above all to point to and usher in a new and more virtuous future. Just as Morris showed us that you could juxtapose a densely figured carpet with a simple English country chair, so his reworkings of the legends of the past and his rich evocations of the English countryside in his designs can work as well alongside a Corbusier chair as a Jacobean table. Perhaps this is why they particularly lend themselves to the eclectic interiors we are evolving today. With his patterns we can summon a leafy wood in June without feeling that we are drowning in our great grandparents' drawing room.

Above and right:
Morris's Honeysuckle *wallpaper, inspired by the plants, gardens and hedgerows around Kelmscott Manor, works just as well in a simple, contemporary setting. It's easy to forget that to their contemporaries, Morris, Burne-Jones, Rossetti and their friends would have appeared a Bohemian lot. Their taste would have seemed unorthodox in its mixing of furniture, fabrics and objects from many different cultural contexts.*

Further Reading

Faulkner, Peter, *Against the Age: An Introduction to William Morris*, London, 1980

Harvey, Charles, and Press, Jon, *William Morris, Design and Enterprise in Victorian Britain*, Manchester, 1991

Henderson, Philip, *William Morris, His Life, Work and Friends*, London, 1967

MacCarthy, Fiona, *William Morris: A Life for Our Time*, London, 1994

Naylor, Gillian (ed.), *William Morris by Himself: Designs and Writings*, New York, 1988

Parry, Linda, *William Morris Textiles*, London, 1983

Parry, Linda (ed.), *William Morris*, London, 1996

Ruskin, John, *The Stones of Venice*, edited and introduced by Jan Morris, London, 1981

Stansky, Peter, *William Morris*, Oxford, 1983

Stansky, Peter, *Redesigning the World: William Morris, the 1880s, and the Arts and Crafts Movement*, Princeton, 1985

Thompson, E.P., *William Morris: Romantic to Revolutionary*, revised edition, London, 1977

Thompson, Paul, *The Work of William Morris*, revised edition, Oxford, 1991

Wilmer, Clive (ed.), *'News From Nowhere' and Other Writings by William Morris*, Hammersmith, 1994

Some of Morris's writings can be found on the internet, through: **www.morrissociety.org** *or* **www.marxists.org/archive/morris**

Picture Credits

Sanderson would like to thank the following stylists and photographers: Caroline Arbour, Julia Bird, Rosie Brown, Siri Hills, Tom Leyton, Ian McManus, Charis White and Polly Wreford. Thanks also to Amanda Graham, Aiva Sarkans and Georgia Metcalfe at Sanderson; and to Austen Thomas and Leo Schofield at Sanderson Brookmill.

Front of jacket: Green room, © Sanderson. Fabric is *Arbutus*; paints shown are *Privet* (walls), *Loden* (skirting) and *Hay* (shutters) by Morris & Co.
Back of jacket: Modern craft roomset, © Sanderson. Courtesy of Andrew Wicks at Contemporary Applied Arts, 2 Percy Street, London W1 1DD. Wallpaper is *Daisy*.
Endpapers: Trial for *Lily* wallpaper, 1874, © Sanderson.
Page ii: Study, © Sanderson. Fabric is *Arbutus*.
Page vii: *Iris* furnishing textile, V&A: T.45–1919.

INTRODUCTION
Page 2: William Morris, c.1875, © Sanderson.
Page 3: *Daisy* wallpaper sample, V&A: E.442–1919.
Page 3: *Fruit* (or *Pomegranate*) wallpaper sample, V&A: E.442–1919.
Page 4: *Larkspur* wallpaper sample, V&A: E.472–1919.

Page 5: Merton Abbey, V&A Museum.
Page 6: *Marigold* furnishing textile, V&A: Circ.496–1965.
Page 7: *Brother Rabbit* printed cotton, V&A: T.647–1919.
Page 7: *Bird and Anemone* wallpaper sample, V&A: E.530–1919.
Page 8: Wallpaper stand book, V&A: E.2734 to 2866–1980.
Page 9: *Acorn* wallpaper, © Sanderson.

CRAFT
Pages 10-11: Embroidery kit detail, V&A: Circ.302–1960.
Page 12: Wallpaper printing block, © Sanderson.
Page 13: Carbrook carpet, V&A: Circ.458–1965.
Page 13: Hand-printing, © Sanderson. Design being printed is *Tulip Frieze*.
Page 14: Morris chairs in interior, © Andrew Wood at *House & Garden*/The Condé Nast Publications Ltd.
Page 14: Hatherleigh pottery courtyard, © Gavin Kingcome for Hatherleigh Pottery, Devon.
Page 15: The conservatory, Emery Walker's house, 7 Hammersmith Terrace, © Cheltenham Art Gallery and Museums.
Page 15: *Primrose* tile, V&A: C.59–1931.
Page 16: *Bullrush* paint room with table, © Sanderson. Ostrich eggs courtesy of Riverwood Ostrich Farm, Finchampstead,

Wokingham, Berkshire, RG40 4QT; Lampshade courtesy of Robert Wyatt, 13 The Shrubbery, Grosvenor Road, London E11 2EL; Coffee cups courtesy of Andrew Wicks at Contemporary Applied Arts, 2 Percy Street, London W1 1DD. Paint is *Bullrush* by Morris & Co.
Page 16: Detail of vase and teapot, © Sanderson. Courtesy of Edmund de Waal at Contemporary Applied Arts, 2 Percy Street, London W1 1DD.
Page 17: as Back of jacket.

COLOUR
Pages 18-19: *Snakeshead* fabric, V&A: T.37–1919.
Page 21: *Honeysuckle* fabric, V&A: Circ.491–1965.
Pages 22-3: Colour palette of gold tones based upon original Morris & Co. wallpapers and fabrics, © Sanderson. Hand-printed wallpapers are *Bird and Anemone* and *Poppy*.
Pages 24-5: Wallpaper log book, © Sanderson.
Pages 26-7: Colour palette of reds and greens, © Sanderson. Hand-printed wallpaper is *Trellis*.
Page 28: Detail of colour buckets, © Sanderson.
Page 29: as Front of jacket.
Pages 30-1: Colour palette of Morris greens, © Sanderson. Hand-printed wallpaper is *Acanthus*.
Pages 32-3: Colour palette of neutral tones, © Sanderson. Hand-printed wallpaper is *Pink and Rose*.

Page 34: White room with embroidered curtains, © Sanderson.
Page 34: *Compton* roomset, © Sanderson. Fabric is *Compton*.
Page 35: Merton Abbey dye book, courtesy of the Huntington Library, Art Collections, and Botanical Gardens, San Marino, California.
Pages 36-7: Colour palette of indigos and reds, © Sanderson. Hand-printed wallpaper is *Apple*.

HONESTY
Pages 38-9: *Sunflower* paper, V&A: E.572–1919.
Page 40: Red House stairwell, © Martin Charles.
Page 41: Red House corridor, © Martin Charles.
Page 42: *Jasmine* roomset, © Sanderson. Fabric is *Jasmine*.
Page 43: Kelmscott Manor chair, © Antony Crolla, *The World of Interiors*.
Page 43: Kelmscott Manor dining table, © Antony Crolla, *The World of Interiors*.
Page 44: Bathroom with Morris tile, © Sanderson. Soap courtesy of Cath Kidston, 6 Clarendon Cross, London W11 4AP.
Page 44: Drawing room at Kelmscott House, © National Portrait Gallery, London.
Page 45: Morris with daughters, © National Portrait Gallery, London.
Page 45: *Garden Tulip* paper, V&A: E.551–1919.

Page 46: Hayes' cottage dining room, © Carolyn L. Bates Photography, Burlington, Vermont, USA.

Page 46: Upstairs hallway, © Sanderson. Wallpaper is *Standen*.

Page 47: Hayes' cottage bedroom, © Sandra Vitzthum Architect, LLC, Montpelier, Vermont, USA. Wallpaper is *Honeysuckle*.

Page 48: Kitchen roomset, © Sanderson. Bowls and basket courtesy of Summerill & Bishop, 100 Portland Road, London W11 4LN. Fabric is *Arbutus*.

Page 48: Kitchen sink, © Sanderson. Paint is *Vellum* by Morris & Co.

Page 49: Hibarigaoka Gakuen, Takarazuka City, Japan, © Katsuhiro Oshima.

PATTERN

Pages 50-1: *Tulip* printed textile, V&A: T.628–1919.

Page 52: *Windrush* curtain, © Sanderson. Fabric is *Windrush*.

Page 53: *Willow Bough* detail, © Sanderson. Wallpaper is *Willow Bough*.

Page 53: *Artichoke* hanging, V&A: T.166–1978.

Page 54: *Trellis* paper, V&A: E.452–1919.

Page 54: Red House exterior, © Martin Charles.

Page 55: *Acanthus* original design, V&A: Circ.297–1955.

Page 56: Dining room of 7 Hammersmith Terrace, © Cheltenham Art Gallery and Museums.

Page 56: Lindsay Kemp's *Fruit* room, © John Ferro Simms for *Country Homes* magazine.

Page 57: Wightwick Manor library, National Trust Photographic Library/Andreas von Einsiedel.

Page 58: *Pink and Rose* roomset, © Barry Dixon Inc. Interior Design. Photographed by Peter Estersohn for *Southern Accents* magazine.

Page 59: Lindsay Kemp's bedroom, © John Ferro Simms for *Country Homes* magazine.

Page 60: *Golden Lily* fireplace roomset, © Sanderson. Morris & Co. chair courtesy of The Millinery Works Gallery Ltd, 85/87 Southgate Road, Islington, London N1 3JS. Wallpaper is *Golden Lily*; fabric is *Iris*.

Page 61: *Golden Lily* flower detail, © Sanderson.

Page 61: Artist's materials, *Golden Lily* roomset. © Sanderson.

NATURE

Pages 62-3: *Strawberry Thief* textile, V&A: T.586–1919.

Page 64: Bench with *Iris* cushion, © Sanderson.

Page 65: *Pimpernel* wallpaper, © Sanderson.

Page 66: *Rose* design, V&A: E.1075–1988.

Page 66: Wallpaper list, © Sanderson.

Page 67: *Blackthorn* roomset, © Sanderson. Fabric is *Blackthorn*; wallpaper is Owen Jones.

Page 67: *Wild Tulip* wallpaper design, V&A: E.538–1919.

Page 68: Standen House and gardens, West Sussex, National Trust Photographic Library/Rupert Truman.

Page 69: Orchard at Standen House, West Sussex, National Trust Photographic Library/Stephen Robson.

Page 70: Kelmscott Manor, © Antony Crolla, *The World of Interiors*.

Page 71: Kelmscott Manor garden, © Antony Crolla, *The World of Interiors*.

Page 71: Kelmscott Manor interior with *Kennet* fabric, © Antony Crolla, *The World of Interiors*.

Page 72: Hayes' cottage in woods, © Carolyn L. Bates Photography, Burlington, Vermont, USA.

Page 73: Hayes' cottage, open door with rose, © Sandra Vitzthum Architect, LLC, Montpelier, Vermont, USA.

Page 73: Garden detail, © Sanderson.

LEGEND

Pages 74-5: *Peacock & Dragon* textile, V&A: T.64–1933.

Page 76: The Oak Room, Wightwick Manor, National Trust Photographic Library/Andreas von Einsiedel.

Page 77: Wightwick Manor Hall, National Trust Photographic Library/Andreas von Einsiedel.

Page 78: *Daisy* hanging, © Antony Crolla, *The World of Interiors*.

Page 79: *Cray* bedroom, © Sanderson. Printed fabric and wallpaper are both *Cray*; red cushions and throw are *Thistle*.

Page 79: *Cray* wallpaper detail, © Sanderson.

Page 80: *Bird and Anemone* roomset, © Sanderson. Curtains are *Bird and Anemone*; wallpaper is *Standen*.

Page 81: Flower/book detail, © Sanderson.

Page 81: Kelmscott Manor tapestry, © Antony Crolla, *The World of Interiors*.

Page 82: Morris in study, © National Portrait Gallery, London.

Page 83: Red House stained-glass quarries, V&A: C.63–1979.

Page 83: Burne-Jones zodiac panel, V&A Museum.

Page 84: *Fruit* 'vintage' roomset, © Sanderson. Coffee cups courtesy of Andrew Wicks at Contemporary Applied Arts, 2 Percy Street, London W1 1DD. Fabric is *Fruit*; paints are *Heather* and *Ivory* by Morris & Co.

Page 84: *Fruit* 'vintage' detail, © Sanderson.

Page 85: *Honeysuckle* details, © Sanderson.

Page 85: *Honeysuckle* 'vintage' study, © Sanderson. Wallpaper is *Honeysuckle*.

Index